A PIG IS BIG

by Douglas Florian

Greenwillow Books
An Imprint of HarperCollinsPublishers

Watercolor paints and colored pencils were used for the full-color art.
The text type is Kabel.

A Pig Is Big.
Copyright © 2000 by Douglas Florian.
All rights reserved. Printed in Singapore by Tien Wah Press.
www.harperchildrens.com

Library of Congress Cataloging-in-Publication Data
Florian, Douglas.
A pig is big / by Douglas Florian.
p.   cm.
"Greenwillow Books."
Summary: Rhyming text explains that cows are bigger than pigs,
cars are bigger still, and the universe is the biggest of all.
ISBN 0-688-17125-7 (trade).   ISBN 0-688-17126-5 (lib. bdg.)
[1. Size—Fiction.   2. Size perception—Fiction.   3. Stories in rhyme.]
I. Title.   PZ8.3F6645 Pi   2000   [E]—dc21   99-053528

1   2   3   4   5   6   7   8   9   10
First Edition

For my daughter
Anael Rachel

What's big?

A pig is big.
A pig is fat.
A pig is bigger than my hat.

What's bigger than a pig?

A cow.
It's bigger than a boar or sow.
It's bigger yesterday and now.

What's bigger than a cow?

A car.
It's bigger than a cow by far.
Inside a car a cow can squeeze
And drive a pig to town with ease.

What's bigger than a car?

A truck.
A truck can haul a car that's stuck,
That's stuck in all the mud—bad luck.

What's bigger than a truck?

A street,
Where trucks and cars and buses meet.
You measure it in miles, not feet.

What's bigger

than a street?

You could . . .
Answer, "It's a neighborhood."
Add streets together, and I'll bet
A neighborhood is what you'll get.

What's bigger

than a neighborhood?

A city, for it's understood
That neighborhoods sit side by side
And help to make a city wide.

What's bigger

than a city?

Well . . .
The earth's dimensions do excel.
In magnitude it is gigantic,
From Katmandu to the Atlantic.

What's bigger than

the whole wide earth?

The universe is wide in girth.
It is the biggest thing of all.

Compared

to it

all things

seem

small.

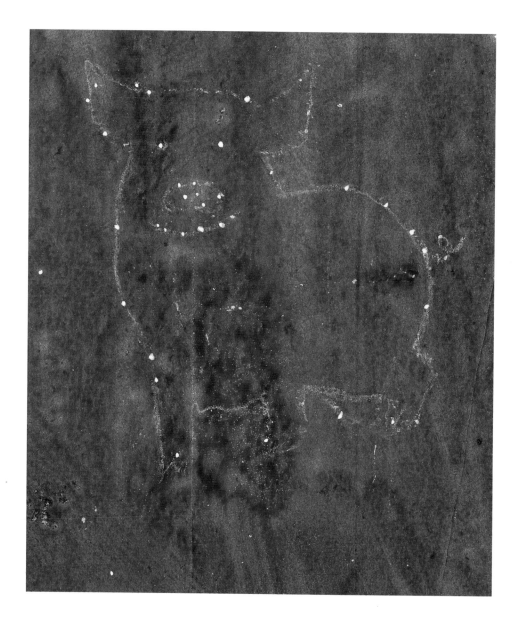